THE LONG CAIRNS OF THE BRECKNOCKSHIRE BLACK MOUNTAINS

By W. F. GRIMES, M.A., F.S.A.

INTRODUCTION.

THIS paper is reprinted from the December, 1936, part of *Archaeologia Cambrensis*, by the kind permission of the Editors of that journal.

In this introduction an attempt is made to expand the description of the general conditions of the time of the megalithic monuments briefly given on page 5, in order that the significance of the Brecknockshire long cairns as part of a wider scheme may be the better appreciated.

For a proper understanding of the movements which spread the " megalithic idea " throughout Europe (as far as understanding is possible in the present incomplete state of knowledge) it is necessary to go back several thousand years before the period 2500–2000 B.C. to which in this country they are generally assigned. The process began in the Near and Middle East, where the development of agriculture and the related arts, and the growth of systems of trade and commerce, had led to the formation of vigorous city-states, which grew rapidly as their prosperity increased. In the third millennium B.C. expansion had become inevitable, and so was set in motion an involved series of movements by which the new ideas were rapidly spread all over Europe.

Of these movements those which brought the megalithic tombs formed one group. But the actual origin of the idea of building tombs of large, generally unhewn stones is still uncertain. A growing opinion sees in the Mediterranean region its most likely place, and in the natural or rock-cut cave its most likely prototype, the idea being that the tombs are an attempt to create artificial caves in built stone in areas where caves did not exist naturally. But in any case, the idea found expression in various ways, and the distributions of the different types show clearly how diverse were the movements by which they were spread. The essentially coastal character of the general distribution is sufficient to show that the megalith-builders travelled mainly by sea : they were in fact the first people to open up the sea-ways of Atlantic Europe. And sufficient is already known of them to enable us to picture the time as one of almost incredible activity, in which the various parts of the British Isles, France, the Mediterranean and Scandinavia were linked together by numberless movements, some local, others more distant in character. (In addition to these, other transcontinental movements affected Britain and in due course made contact with the megaliths. They have their origin in the same set of conditions.)

An examination of the megalithic tombs of Wales, although this country cannot claim to have been amongst the richest and most vigorous of the time, illustrates well the extent of the variations. Such an examination obviously could not be attempted here, and the reader interested is therefore referred to the surveys mentioned on page 5. Two essential facts should however be noticed.

In the first place, amongst all the variations, two main groups or series can be recognised.

The first occurs almost entirely in the west. Only scattered monuments apparently belonging to it occur east of Gower in South Wales, while in the north it is confined almost entirely to Merioneth, the Lleyn Peninsula and Anglesey. This series is composed not of one type, but of a number ; and just as its distribution suggests that it is due to oversea movements, so the forms of the monuments, and sometimes the finds from them, enable them to be traced to related monuments in other of the coastal areas of western and southern Europe. Every consideration therefore justifies the title of Western Megalithic Group for this series.

The second group occurs almost entirely in the south coastal plain as far west as Gower, and in the Black Mountains, with an odd pair of monuments in the Conwy Valley of North Wales. Here the monuments are of much more uniform type, for whatever the shape of the chambers themselves—and examination of the plans which follow will show how varied these can be—the most complete invariably have long cairns. The resemblance of this South-eastern Group to the very large series of chambered cairns in the Cotswold area is emphasised on page 20, and suggests that the colonisation of Wales by the megalith-builders was a dual process working from west and east alike.

Until more excavation has been carried out some of the most important problems presented by the long cairns must remain unsolved, and the exact relationships of the different tombs are bound to be uncertain. The only way of advance lies through more complete knowledge of the structure of the tombs, for comparison with others elsewhere, and of the material in them for dating purposes. Here it must be sufficient to emphasise the importance of the Black Mountains long cairns as the largest group of their type in Wales, and as one of the most hopeful means of learning about the " Neolithic " culture of which they formed part—the more so because as yet no settlement-sites of this period have been recognised in South Wales.

The second point to be observed is that on present evidence all the megalithic tombs which have been excavated are broadly speaking of the same date, that is, they belong probably to the centuries on either side of 2000 B.C. The material which has so far been found has not yet made it possible to arrange the tombs in any kind of chronological sequence, although it is quite conceivable that as more work is done—and provided it is done properly—some such sequence may be evolved.

It is perhaps desirable to add that the association of megaliths with the Druids is no longer accepted by responsible archaeological opinion. Excavation within and beyond Wales has long established the general facts of their origin, date and purpose. In an attempt to make this clear the indeterminate name *cromlech* so commonly used in Wales has been discarded throughout this paper in favour of " tomb " and its combinations, which have some relation to the use to which the monuments were put.

I should like to take the opportunity, inadvertantly missed when the paper was first published, of thanking my friend, Mr. L. D. Thomas, for his very kind help in carrying out the field-work. Most of the photographs used in the paper are his.

W. F. G.

THE LONG CAIRNS OF THE BRECKNOCKSHIRE BLACK MOUNTAINS.

THE first recognition of the megalithic monuments of the Black Mountains as a group was due to Mr. O. G. S. Crawford, by whom descriptions of the known examples (including several hitherto unrecorded ones) were published in 1925 in *The Long Barrows of the Cotswolds*. Since 1925 the number of sites has been increased only by one, from 12 to 13. To a great extent, therefore, this paper[1] can only be a repetition of what Mr. Crawford has already written as far as the sites themselves are concerned ; but I have taken this opportunity of publishing a complete series of plans, where the present state of the monuments enables plans to be prepared, and I have also given more attention to the setting of the group than was possible for Mr. Crawford, whose attention was occupied mainly with their neighbours and relatives, the chambered tombs of the Cotswolds.

As I have already summarised elsewhere[2] the main features of the megalithic monuments of Wales, here by way of introduction I must content myself with a map (Fig. 1) which will serve as a reminder of their coastal distribution, and of the anomalous position of the Black Mountains long cairns as the only inland series of any size. It remains to note that the monuments themselves present a variety of type in keeping with the manifold character of the movements of their builders, which are but one manifestation of the unrest and expansion that affected the greater part of Europe in the third millennium B.C. ; and that the Brecknockshire long cairns form part of what I have called a south-eastern group, which does not appear to be *directly* related to the western megaliths, whether of north or south Wales, and whose nearest immediate parallels are provided by the Cotswold long cairns described by Mr. Crawford.

I shall return later to the unusual presence of megalithic tombs so far inland in Wales. Of the Black Mountains themselves I need only

[1] Its substance formed part of a lecture delivered at the Annual Meeting of the Cambrian Archaeological Association at Abergavenny in 1936.

[2] *Proceedings of the Prehist. Society*, 1936, 106–39 (Re-issued as a Museum publication by the National Museum of Wales.) See also the Ordnance Survey *Map of South Wales showing the Distribution of Long Barrows*, etc., which gives fuller details of position, etc., for individual sites in south Wales. A similar map for north Wales is being prepared.

say that they consist of an upland mass of Old Red Sandstone, defined on the south by the River Usk, on the east, north, and

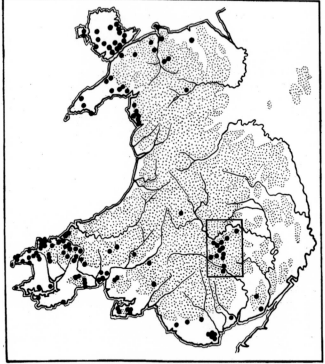

Fig. 1.—Map of Wales showing distribution of Chambered Tombs.
(The area enclosed in the rectangle is shown enlarged in Fig. 2.)

north-east by the Wye and its tributary, the Llynfi. On the south-east the plateau is split up by steep-sided valleys, formed finger-wise by streams belonging to both systems. On the north, the Wye

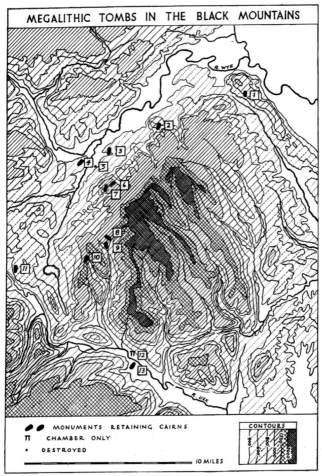

Fig. 2.

Valley is more open, and the steep northward-facing scarp of the mountains has between it and the valley-bottom a zone of foot-hills, spurs, and undulating country dissected by comparatively small streams, and ranging in height from about 400 to 1000 ft. above sea-level.

Examination of the distribution map given in Fig. 2 is sufficient to show—subject always, of course, to the possibility of new discoveries—that the megalith-builders chose the north-western aspect for their main area of settlement. And the string of monuments which extends up the Usk Valley and by way of the Rhiangoll to the Talgarth region further suggests that colonisation took place by way of the Usk, rather than by way of the Wye.

A further obvious point which presents itself from the map is the complete avoidance of the higher upland : a feature which has been observed to be more or less constant throughout Wales. This fact has an obvious bearing upon the problem of the megalith-builders and their environment. For whatever the position in coastal areas, where sea winds may have helped to restrict the forest which was one of early man's greatest difficulties, in an inland region like that of the Black Mountains we have to deal with valleys in which conditions of water, shelter, and soil may all have been favourable to luxuriant vegetation.

To even the most superficial observer it must be obvious that our country to-day, in spite of centuries of intensive agriculture, still supports a very considerable woodland. The character of much of this has no doubt been modified by human activity, but in several places it is possible to detect areas which seem to carry the remains of the original natural forest-growth.

Particularly significant in this respect is the area known as The Forest, at the head of the Rhiangoll Valley, which separates the main mass of the Black Mountains from a western outlier formed of two hills, Mynydd Troed and Mynydd Llangors.

The Forest boasts two monuments, one of which, Tŷ Isaf (9) is obviously a long cairn. (The second, Cwm Fforest (8) I am less happy about, but for this see below.) Tŷ Isaf stands on a small knoll in the angle made by the meeting of two streams at a height of about 850 ft. above sea-level (Figs. 3, 4). To east and west the ground rises steadily, to the former to 2000, to the latter to about 1900 ft. To the north is the ridge which separates the Wye and the Usk river-systems, and the highest point of which (1476 ft.) is the knoll upon which stands the earthwork known as Castell Dinas. The southward-facing slopes of the knoll from about 1200 ft. downwards, still bear extensive patches of what can hardly be other than primeval woodland.[1]

Here, then, we have an instance of a long cairn with apparently natural woodland rising 400–500 ft. above it. And the important

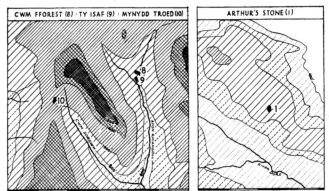

Fig. 3.—Maps showing the siting of Brecknockshire Long Cairns.

point to be noted is that there is no apparent difference in the character of the subsoil in the wooded area and in that which is now

[1] Comparison of the present extent of this woodland with that shown on the 1905 edition of the 6 in. Ordnance Map suggests that there has been much reduction in its extent in recent years, and this is supported by the presence of stools of large trees which may still be seen in the clearings. The upper and steeper slopes carry mainly hazel coppice, with some hawthorn, etc., and alder in wet places. Lower down, where the slope flattens, alder is very abundant, with many trees 30–40 ft. high ; hawthorn and holly persist, and there is also a good deal of bramble and briar. Large trees are comparatively rare, having apparently been felled ; of these ash is commonest; there are some maples, a little birch, and a few oaks. Samples of the last have been identified by Mr. H. A. Hyde, Keeper of the Department of Botany in the National Museum of Wales, as belonging to both common oak (*Quercus Robur* Linnaeus) and hybrids (*Q. petraea* × *Robur*). The evidence suggests an ash-oakwood association in which the more valuable trees have been removed, and the felling of the alders is now gradually increasing the clearings ; but I hasten to add that this suggestion is only offered tentatively, pending examination by a competent botanist.

clear of timber. Moreover, the protection afforded to the lower slopes of the valley by the high ground would have provided an additional encouragement for vegetation. The only conclusion possible seems to be that the Tŷ Isaf long cairn, which is at a level corresponding with that of the lower part of our wooded area, could only have been built after some clearance of woodland had taken place. Of the character of this woodland we cannot, of course, be

Fig. 4.—Tŷ Isaf Long Cairn : View from South-East, showing position.

sure on present evidence ; but in view of the damp conditions attested by the abundance of alder referred to in the footnote we shall not be surprised to find that further research decides in favour of something resembling "damp oakwood."

A cursory examination suggests that patches of woodland similar to that described still exist elsewhere in the Black Mountains, and study of them might be profitable to botanists and archaeologists alike. In any case, it seems likely that what is true of Tŷ Isaf applies to a greater or less extent to most of the other sites at present known. (Gwernvale (12) and Carn Goch (13) are the exceptions, for these, though valley sites (Fig. 5) are shown by the one inch

geological map to be on river-gravel (terrace) and sand respectively—
although this is not to imply that even these positions were quite
" open.") Mynydd Troed (10), at a height of about 1200 ft., in the
saddle between Mynydd Troed and Mynydd Llangors, where its
bracken-free surface stands out in an area otherwise completely
bracken-covered, may have been in the belt of scrub which would
presumably have intervened between the woodland and the open
country ; and the exposed position of Tŷ Illtyd (11) at 800 ft. may
have helped to keep its surroundings more open than would have
been normal to its altitude (Fig. 5).. But if we set our natural

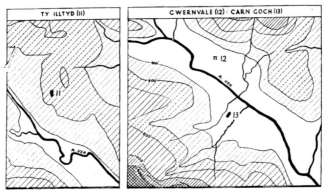

Fig. 5.—Maps showing siting of Brecknockshire Long Cairns.

tree-line at 1200 ft. and ignore the possibilities implied by the
existence in peat of remains of birch and oak 2000 ft. up on the
mountain top (Pen-y-gader Fawr),[1] all our sites lie below, and in most
cases well below, this level. Arthur's Stone (1) (Fig. 3) and the
Ffostill Cairns (6, 7) (Figs. 6, 7) are on open level or slightly sloping

[1] The date of these deposits has not of course been fixed. The adze of Wiltshire
chert published by Wheeler (*Prehistoric and Roman Wales*, p. 61) unfortunately
cannot be used for this purpose, as it was found, so Mr. G. E. Blundell informs me, already lying on the rock floor of a channel cut in the peat, and its relationship to it is
therefore uncertain. This is the more unfortunate because the adze is of a type
which could be accepted as generally contemporary with the megaliths, occurring as
it does in some numbers in the Graig Lwyd axe factory on Penmaen-mawr.

sites at heights of about 800 and 1000 ft. respectively. Pen-y-wyrlod
(2) (Fig. 6) is at 900 ft. on one of the irregular spurs of the Black
Mountains, on rough ground unsuited for agriculture, which supports
a retrogressive woodland. Little Lodge (3) and Pipton (4) are
between 400 and 500 ft., the former on gently sloping ground above a
small tributary of the Wye, the latter on the tip of a spur above the
junction of the Wye and the Llynfi (Fig. 6). The surroundings of the

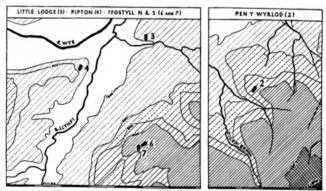

Fig. 6.—Maps showing siting of Brecknockshire Long Cairns.

last two are still well-wooded[1], and somewhere hereabouts must also
have been Croesllechau (5), although its exact position is not known.
Finally, Cwm Fforest (8) (Fig. 3) is actually in the lower part of the
Castell Dinas woodland ; but its unusual character is such that
pending some kind of test excavation, I should prefer not to base any
conclusions upon it.

[1] As the photographs (Figs. 8, 9) show, large oaks flourish on Pipton to-day, and
there are many more in the locality. Out of 15 specimens collected, 14 were identified
by Mr. Hyde as Common Oak (Q. Robur L.), the single remaining specimen as
Durmast Oak (Q. petraea Liebl.). It is not, of course, suggested that these trees are
the remnants of a " natural woodland." The implication is that an area which
supports such trees to-day would have supported woodland in the more favourable
conditions of the past.

The main conclusion to be drawn from this survey seems to be that we have here a valley movement which is not a chance adventure of a few individuals—the general possibility that neolithic man may have cleared woodland in some places has long been widely accepted—but rather a deliberate colonisation by settlers who consistently avoided the higher ground. The nature of the obstacles

Fig. 7.—View of the Ffostill Long Cairns from the South-East.

to be overcome in such a movement would naturally vary according to local conditions : a high-level plateau would hardly be expected to present the same resistance as a low-lying knoll, spur, or valley-side. But it is idle here to attempt distinctions which will only be possible after detailed study of the environmental factors, even if present indications lead us to suspect—as I have already suggested—that at their worst the conditions must have approximated to those of " damp oakwood." The reasons for this policy may perhaps be found in the fact that the long cairn people were agriculturists (although at the moment we have no very satisfactory evidence of this from Wales), who avoided the upland as unsuited for their mode of life.

Evidence of date may be more conveniently considered after we have examined the condition and character of the monuments themselves.

This stage in our survey must open with a warning. We shall see presently that the chambers of several of our cairns have been

Fig. 8.—Pipton Long Cairn : View from East.

excavated, but the cairns themselves have not been touched. Excavation of monuments of this type in recent years has frequently revealed an unexpected complexity and variety of form which has completely changed their character ; but heie we are entirely dependent upon the weathered and mutilated outward state of cairns and chambers, and we have always, therefore, to face the probability that excavation will materially modify views which we are compelled to base upon incomplete, if not actually upon misleading evidence. This evidence is summarised in the series of plans, Figs. 14–20.

At best, therefore, the cairns can only be said to be oval or egg-shaped, without prejudice as to their original form.[1] The commonest form appears to be wider and higher at one end than the other[2]—Pen-y-wyrlod, Pipton, Ffostill North and South, and Mynydd Troed all show this feature. But Ffostill South is more squat and almost rectangular, and this is true also of Tŷ Illtyd, although here the cairn

Fig. 9.—Pipton Long Cairn : View of the wider north end, showing the two stones of the main chamber which remain above the ground.   Their un-symmetrical position is perhaps due to " spread " of the cairn down the slope.

may have suffered from a tendency to " spread " down the hill-side. hence, perhaps, the un-symmetrical position of the chamber within it.

[1] The impossibility of coming to a definite decision from such remains will be apparent to anyone who will compare Ward's final plan of the Tinkinswood, Glamorgan, long cairn with that made before excavation (*Arch. Camb.*, 1915–16). The latter gave no hint of the rectangularity (actually slight wedge-shape) of the former.

[2] Where the " broad " end can be distinguished either in the plan of the cairn or by the presence of the main chamber, it is represented by the shape of the symbol on the map.   Other cairns are shown oval.

Without exception, the cairns have suffered mutilation : sometimes, as at Ffostill, their outlines have been further modified by ploughing, and all of them have been dug into or denuded for stone.   At Little Lodge quarrying has almost completely obliterated part of the cairn, and at Arthur's Stone the effect of the close proximity of hedges and a road combined has been to produce an irregular oval affair which (particularly because of the unusual character of the chamber)

Fig. 10.—The main (i.e. East) chamber of Ffostill North Long Cairn, from the West.

provides no evidence as to the original shape of the cairn.   There is much variation in size.   Little Lodge is thought to have been 200 ft. long ; Ffostill North and Pipton (Figs. 8, 9), which are much better preserved, are about 130 ft. long, 70 and 80 ft. wide, and 8 and 6 ft. high respectively.   At the other end of the scale comes Pen-y-wyrlod, 52–5 ft. by 30, with little more than a skin of stones remaining.   The outlines of even the best preserved cairns are frequently difficult to distinguish within a few feet either way.

Their alignment follows no fixed rule.

The cairns normally have what may be called a main chamber in the broader end (where this can be distinguished), and there are usually " secondary chambers " (the term is used without prejudice as to their date) in the longer sides, and even sometimes in the opposite end, but these are often represented only by single stones which show above the surface of the cairn. Even the main chambers tend to be small and cist-like in appearance (Fig. 10) : Pen-y-wyrlod, for example, is only 6 by 4 ft. But others are longer and passage-

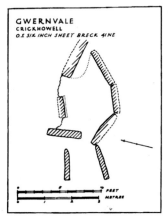

Fig. 11.—Gwernvale Burial Chamber : Plan.

like, as in the main chamber of Ffostill South, and the side-chamber of Tŷ Isaf, with its entrance at one corner. Ffostill North, on the other hand, has a small box-like cist on its north side.

Gwernvale, the one monument in the group which has lost its cairn, is almost certainly a secondary chamber of polygonal type, with short passage-approach which is partly closed by a cross-slab (Fig. 11). The form suggests relationship with similar chambers in some of the Cotswold long cairns.

Two monuments are exceptional : Tŷ Illtyd and Arthur's Stone. The chamber of the former is un-symmetrically placed in its mound, which, as already stated, has probably suffered both from " spread " and mutilation. The complete plan cannot be recovered without excavation ; but what remains (Figs. 12, 20) is sufficient to show that the chamber was more elaborate than usual, with the possibility that it is related to the passage-grave-with-transepts type of the Cotswolds. At the same time, this comparison cannot be pressed.

Arthur's Stone seems to be unique. I have already stated my opinion that the form of the cairn has been too much altered to be

Fig. 12.—Ty Illtyd Long Cairn : View of remains of chamber from North.

admitted as evidence. The chamber is far larger than any other in the group, and Mr. Hemp has rightly, I think, pointed out that the shape of the capstone has dictated the arrangement of the supports ;[1] but the true abnormality lies in the peculiar angled passage, for which no parallel appears to be forthcoming.

[1] *Arch. Camb.*, 1935, 288–92. At the same time, I cannot agree with his reconstruction purporting to show stones now fallen or leaning in their original positions. Unless the outlines of actual holes are visible (and I must confess that I could not discover any) I do not see how these positions are to be fixed without excavation to determine the depth of the stone in the ground.

It may or may not be significant that both of these unusual monuments lie away from the main area of settlement as at present known. Arthur's Stone in particular suggests localised development of the long cairn form, which might be expected to happen in more remote areas at a comparatively late date.

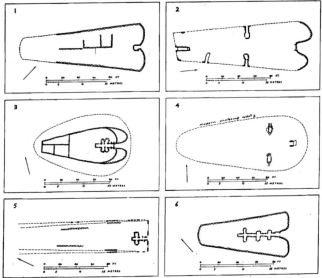

Fig. 13.—Comparative Series of Plans of Cotswold Long Cairns. (1) Randwick ; (2) Belas Knap ; (3) Hetty Pegler's Tump ; (4) Windmill Tump, Rodmarton ; (5) Wayland's Smithy ; (6) Stoney Littleton.

(1, after Crawford, *Long Barrows* ; 2, after Kendrick and Hawkes, *Archaeology*, Fig. 27; 3, after Thurnham in *Archaeologia*, XLII ; 4, after Thurnham in *Crania Britannica*, II ; 5, after Peers and Smith in *Antiq. Journ.*, 1921 ; 6, after Balch, *Wookey Hole.*)

We have now to consider the date and source of the movement which these long cairns attest. As to the latter, there can, I think, be no reasonable doubt that the Brecknockshire monuments are closely related to those of the Cotswolds, whatever the ultimate source of the Cotswold long cairns may be. The series of comparative plans here presented (Fig. 13) displays features most of which are known, though less completely owing to the absence of excavation, in the Brecknockshire group. They are sufficient to show that both belong to the same movement, even if we cannot, in the absence of

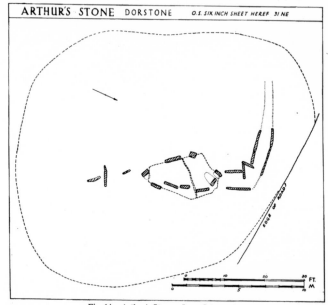

Fig. 14.—Arthur's Stone: Long Cairn : plan.

evidence, decide whether they were independent, or whether (as I personally suspect) the Brecknockshire group is an offshoot of those of the Cotswolds. The solution to the problem of origins is only to be found in comparative studies over a wide area like that now being undertaken by Mr. Glyn Daniel : I can only say that my own reading of the evidence for Wales suggests that there is no sound justification for assuming that the south-eastern group of long cairns, to which

our Brecknockshire series belongs, is related directly to any of the
tombs of West Wales.   The movement which brought them touched
the shores of the Bristol Channel, and penetrated, probably up the
Usk Valley, inland.   But it seems to have ignored the western areas
of megalithic concentration, for nowhere west of Gower in the south,
and away from the Conwy Valley in the north, do we meet with long
cairns incorporating all the features which have been summarised
in this paper.

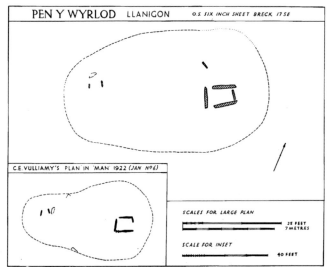

Fig. 15.—Pen-y-Wyrlod Long Cairn : plans showing present conditions and arrangement
at time of excavation.

For the problem of date, two lines of approach are open.   The
first, and less reliable, is that of the form of the tombs themselves ;
the second, the finds made in them.

The tendency to regard the Brecknockshire group as a comparatively late one has been due to two factors.   On the one hand, a
climatic change at the end of the third millennium B.C. which opened

up the interior of the country by reducing the forest-covering has been cited as the factor which enabled them to penetrate so deeply inland. Secondly, the tombs themselves have been thought to be of a " transitional " type, in which the chamber with a structural entrance which could be opened and closed as necessary was replaced by " closed " cists of large size in which burials were inserted by lifting the capstone, on the analogy of certain of the Scandinavian tombs.

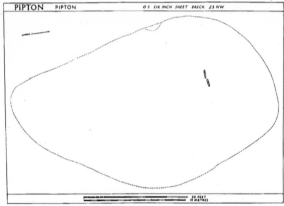

Fig. 16.—Pipton Long Cairn : plan.

As to the first of these arguments, we have already seen that long cairns in our area occur below the present limit of natural woodland ; and since there is no evidence that the tree-line was lower in neolithic times than it is to-day, we can only conclude that the megalith-builders need not have waited for climatic changes to carry out clearings which they were capable of making for themselves.

As to the second, it may be urged that " closed " cists are not perhaps so prevalent in our area as has been thought. With certain of the tombs, indeed, provision for an entrance in the normal mega-lithic fashion is definite and obvious. The peculiar entrance passage of Arthur's Stone has already been mentioned ; the elaboration of

Tŷ Illtyd is hardly in keeping with a closed cist; the secondary chamber of Tŷ Isaf was entered at its south-west corner; Gwernvale has a wholly characteristic short entrance-passage; and Pen-y-wyrlod, though in its present form shown closed, on Mr. Vulliamy's plan prepared at the time of excavation displays an opening in its east side which may quite well be provision for an entrance.

Even with apparently closed cists as represented at Ffostill (Figs. 10, 17), we cannot be sure of their true character until one or more

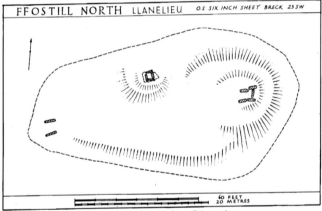

Fig. 17.—Ffostill North Long Cairn : plan.
(Based on C. E. Vulliamy in *Arch. Camb.*, 1923.)

of the sites has been adequately explored. The north secondary chamber of Ffostill North is certainly of the small size and box-like shape which we should expect such a cist to assume; but the main chambers of both cairns have their cross-slabs set back to suggest a portal (pottery and bones were actually found outside one of them, as elsewhere in the forecourts of long cairns—see below), and only excavation of the *cairn* can decide whether or not provision was made by means of horns or a dry-stone passage for entrance to them. This has not yet been done.

Of 7 monuments complete enough to rank as evidence, therefore, two may (or may not) employ the " closed cist " idea. The remainder have more or less well-defined provision for entrance from the end or side in normal megalithic style. So that the evidence of typology hardly supports the idea that these long cairns as a group are to be treated as late and transitional. We must rather agree that (as we should expect) at most we have to deal with features of varying date which express the changes in ideas and practice that took place during the life of the megalithic cult in our area.

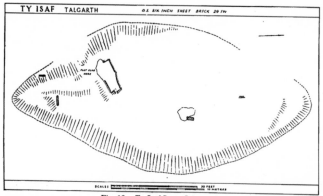

Fig. 18.—Ty Isaf Long Cairn : plan.

The admittedly uncertain evidence provided by external factors and typology is confirmed by the scanty datable finds recovered from excavation.[1] (In passing it should be noted that the chambers explored have all produced quantities of human remains, indicating continued use as burial vaults, though perhaps not for complete bodies at time of death ; and that in some instances it has been possible to recognise these as of the long-headed " neolithic " type.)

[1] For Mr. Vulliamy's excavation reports see as follows : *Ffostill—Arch. Camb.*, 1921, 300 ff. ; 1923, 320–4. *Pen-y-wyrlod—Arch. Camb.*, 1921, 296–7 (Marshall and Morgan) ; *Man.*, 1922, No. 6. *Little Lodge—Man.*, 1929, No. 20.

The finds of importance consist of :—

(1) Fragments of a round-bottomed bowl, probably of Neolithic A type, found just outside the chamber of Ffostill South, where it was associated with human remains.[1] No part of the rim or other distinctive feature has survived.

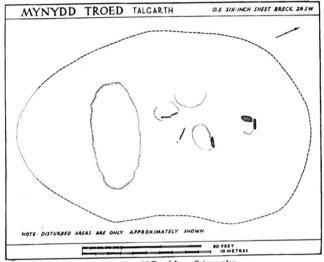

Fig. 19.—Mynydd Troed Long Cairn : plan.

(2) Fragments of beaker pottery, from the chamber of Pen-y-wyrlod. The form is quite uncertain, but pieces of characteristic base can be recognised. The decoration consists of fingernail impressions.

(3) Fragments of heavier pottery of Bronze Age type, from the northern side-chamber of Ffostill North. Again the fragments are too small to determine form. They are possibly part of a cinerary urn.

[1] The depth of the find is not stated.

The first two conclusively indicate that some at any rate of the Brecknockshire long cairns are broadly contemporary with those elsewhere. Finds of both neolithic and beaker pottery are normal to megaliths throughout the country, for the beaker people undoubtedly made contacts with the megalith-builders, and their pottery occurs

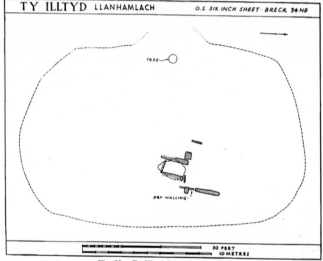

Fig. 20.—Ty Illtyd Long Cairn : plan.

sometimes in primary association (i.e. it belongs to the time of the first erection and use of the tomb), sometimes in secondary deposits. The body of material available at the present time does not enable us to attempt any closer chronological classification. (3), on the other hand, suggests that the use of the tomb may have gone on until a comparatively late date, just as Bronze Age barrows enjoyed a prolonged life—it will be recalled that a Bronze Age barrow in the same field beside the long cairns is evidence for later occupation of the area—and it is even possible (although this does not seem to have been considered at the time of excavation) that the chamber itself may have been a late insertion.

From this brief survey of the Black Mountains long cairns the following points therefore emerge :—

(1) They represent a movement the immediate origin of which may have been the Cotswolds, and which probably penetrated to Brecknockshire by way of the Usk Valley.

(2) The movement was essentially a valley-movement. The megalith-builders avoided the upland as being probably un-suited to their mode of life, and they seem to have possessed the necessary means of overcoming the various types of natural woodland which occurred in the valleys between the 400 and 1200 ft. contours, where their sites are placed.

(3) The long cairns themselves, although they are very incompletely known, show features which can be paralleled most closely amongst the Cotswold cairns. It may be doubted if there is any justification for the assumption that they are typologically late when compared with long cairns elsewhere.

(4) The evidence of date so far recovered suggests that the earliest examples are broadly contemporary with other long cairns. That they should be slightly later is natural in view of their position ; the difference, however, is not that implied between " neolithic " and " early Bronze Age." Sometimes, at least, they may have continued in use until a comparatively late date.

The uncertain character of some of these conclusions is a measure of the necessity for thorough scientific excavation of one or more members of the group.

APPENDIX : NOTES ON MONUMENTS NOT ILLUSTRATED BY PLANS.

The plans here published are new, with the exception of that of Ffostill North, which is based on Mr. Vulliamy's plan in *Arch. Camb.*, 1923, and which I have re-published because it illustrates all the features of its type in their best state of preservation. Ffostill South has also been published by Mr. Vulliamy, and re-publication was clearly unnecessary. (The plans are reproduced on a uniform scale, except that the larger cairns (Ffostill North and Pipton) have been reduced to half the size of the smaller ones for reasons of space.)

Four sites are not illustrated.

Little Lodge (3) has been so much mutilated by quarrying that its complete plan cannot be recovered. More or less ruined chambers at the middle and south (narrow) end of the cairn were excavated by Mr. Vulliamy and produced human bones but no datable finds. (*Man.*, 1929, No. 20.)

Croesllechau (5) is now destroyed. Its position is fairly closely known from early maps. (Crawford, *Long Barrows*, 53–4.)

Cwm Fforest (8) consists of a drystone-walled chamber 8 by 6 ft., in what appears to be a small cairn (orientated south-east-north-west) defined on one side by a deep gully, and directly above the Rhiangoll river. The chamber has a channel-like passage, partly covered by a flat slab, leading from its south-east side. The arrangement is peculiar, and as the site is much overgrown some kind of clearing seems to be desirable before its true character can be decided.

Carn Goch (13) is a very much ruined long cairn in Llangattock Park. Its apparently round character is deceptive, and due to the almost complete destruction of its " tail," of which only faint traces remain. It seems to have had a length of about 80 ft. and width of 50–60 ft., but no other distinctive features of importance remain.

Lightning Source UK Ltd.
Milton Keynes UK
176211UK00001B/62/P